Louisiana State University Press    Baton Rouge and London

# Eden *Aceh's Rainforest*

*Text & photographs by Michael Griffiths*

Photographs & text © Michael Griffiths
Editor: Gregory Vitiello
Art director & designer: Derek Birdsall
Production: Martin Lee
Printed in England by Penshurst Press

© Mobil Services Co. Ltd.

First published in the United States, 1990
by Louisiana State University Press
Baton Rouge, Louisiana 70893

ISBN 0–8071–1615–7

A friend of the University who wishes to remain anonymous
has generously assisted in the publication of this volume.

# Contents

# *Foreword*

MENTERI NEGARA
KEPENDUDUKAN DAN LINGKUNGAN HIDUP

Indonesia has been particularly graced in the wealth and beauty of its rainforests. They are certainly one of our national treasures: home to much of our wildlife and plant life, and the source of life in the very air we breathe. It is therefore essential that we treat our rainforests as treasures.

This book, which depicts the beauty and variety of one Acehnese rainforest, serves a much-needed purpose. It reminds us of what we could too easily lose and what we should value more.

Michael Griffiths, who has put his passion and his talent to work in photographing the rainforest, deserves our special thanks. So too does Mobil Oil Indonesia, which has backed his enterprise for the past three years.

Let us now follow their example and reinvigorate our efforts to keep the rainforest alive.

Jakarta, August 1, 1989

*Emil Salim*
Minister of State
for Population and Environment
Republic of Indonesia

## *Acknowledgements*

This book could never have been created without the generous patronage of Mobil Oil Indonesia, which had the vision to back my idea before concern for the rainforest became widespread. I would especially like to thank Les Cargile for his foresight, as well as Kent Acord, who added his support at critical times. I am also grateful to Ray Vaughan, Ariono Suriawinata and K. I. Mahmud for their advice and support.

For their work in processing visas and permits and otherwise grappling with the various bureaucracies, I am indebted to Adnan Madewa of the Ford Foundation and to Dr. Linus Simanjuntak of Yayasan Indonesia Hijau.

It would be impossible to name all the people who extended their hospitality to me during my travels, but I would like especially to thank Ryne and Kristin Palombit and Peter Assink and Iris Van Dyk at the Ketambe Research Station and Richard and Carol Northrip at Bukit Indah. Also, Pak Ali at Ladang Rimba was not only a fine host but introduced me to many experts in jungle lore.

Considerable technological innovation was required in order to photograph the more elusive animals, and without the enthusiastic support of Jeffrey Low and Goh of Olympus Optical and Eugene Gan of Showa Arco, no tigers would have graced these pages.

I would like also to thank Lita Sulaiman who transformed my "hieroglyphics" into a legible draft, and also David Heckman and Ed Van Ness whose material support and encouragement were invaluable.

Finally, to my companions in the forest—Pak Yusuf, the elephant lover of north Aceh; Bangun, the primate research assistant at Ketambe and, most of all, Samsul, Gadi and Mohammad Alamshah, who shared with me more than 280 campfires—I am forever grateful for your forbearance, good humor, skill and courage.

# Preface

Traditionally, tropical rainforests have been depicted as dangerous and forbidding places—dense green wildernesses that are the abode of poisonous snakes, ferocious carnivores, killer fish and plagues of insects. Although there is a grain of truth behind these notions, it is only part of the picture. The forests are in fact vitally productive systems that contain an astonishing diversity of life, both floral and faunal, and there is much that is not only harmless, but that is also sublimely beautiful. Increasingly too, we are learning how much there is that is of use and value to man.

This book is an attempt to redress the bias and to give a balanced portrayal of life in the rainforests of Sumatra and in particular those in the province of Aceh. These forests are as rich as any on earth, and are home to animals familiar to people the world over—elephants, rhinos, tigers, bears and that close relative of man, the orang-utan.

Diversity of life should not be confused with abundance, and many first-time visitors to South East Asia's rainforests are surprised at how few large animals they see in comparison, say, to the savannas of Africa or the terai of Nepal. This scarcity, together with the limited visibility resulting from the dense vegetation, makes photography frustratingly difficult. Only by spending more than two years in the forests was I able to produce the photographs that appear in this book.

During this time, I and my team had to overcome many real difficulties—sickness, broken bones, crippling insect stings, flooded rivers and even starvation. Some of the wildlife damaged the very equipment that was intended to record it; tigers, bears, rats, ants and termites all chewed on camera gear, elephants just crushed it. Even the warm air took its toll by nurturing a filamental fungus that spread over electronics and optics alike. Eventually there were successes, but the trials, frustrations, adventures and observations form the story around which this book is based.

Sumatra's forests, like those in many other places, are fast diminishing. If the current trend continues, some of the animals pictured here will be so rare that they will be virtually impossible to photograph three years from now. So this volume constitutes a testament to those forests and a plea for their preservation.

About 75,000 years ago an awesome eruption shook the very foundations of the land where Sumatra lies today. The size of the cataclysm defies the imagination; indeed, nothing in recorded history even comes close. It was 1,500 times as great as the recent eruption of Mount St. Helens in North America, spewing ash as far away as India and probably altering the world's climate for years afterward. After the dust had settled, the land lay bare. At the center was a crater almost 80 kilometers long where the subterranean forces had blasted through the earth's crust.

For all its size, this eruption was merely a surface manifestation of even greater forces operating inside the earth. For tens of millions of years, the floor of the Indian Ocean has been thrusting beneath Sumatra. The land has been forced upwards and buckled into the mountain chain that runs the length of the island. Molten rock deep within the earth has forced its way through weak spots and blown out at the surface as volcanoes, several of which are still active today.

In time, the wounds of the great eruption healed. The crater filled with water to form the beautiful Lake Toba, and the desolate land turned green as trees and plants spread from the vast forests to the east.

The Sumatra of today is just one part of what was once a great expanse of land extending southeast from what are now Malaysia and Indochina. The islands of Palawan, Borneo, Bali, Java and Sumatra define the outer limits of this ancient subcontinent called Sundaland. For two million years this land went through alternating periods of emergence and inundation in response to successive ice ages. The lowlands of Sundaland were spared the freezing conditions of the higher latitudes, however; and secure within an equable climate, forests of extraordinary richness and diversity flourished. They were the product of over 100 million years of natural development, and to them, animals came from some of the farthest regions of the earth. Rhinos that may have originated in Europe found their way here; the elephant and hippopotamus whose ancestors may have evolved in Africa came also; and the tapir, known outside this region only in South and Central America, found conditions ideal. Later still, tigers came, perhaps beginning their journey in grasslands north of China. And last of all, about 40,000 years ago, came modern man.

About 10,000 years ago the earth's climate ameliorated somewhat. The ice sheets began to melt and the resulting rise in sea level flooded the lowlands of Sundaland, successively separating the islands of Bali, Java, Borneo and finally Sumatra from the Asian mainland. Yet Sundaland's ancient connection with Asia lingers on to this day. The forests of Borneo, Sumatra and the Malaysian peninsula have many similar flora; the trumpeting of elephants still echoes in the forests of Sumatra, through to India; and the tiger, until recently found also in Java and Bali, still graces the remoter parts of Sumatra as it does in all the countries west, to the foothills of the Himalayas and north to Siberia.

Of the Sundaland relics that remain as islands, Sumatra is perhaps the most richly endowed in natural products. Its varied geography, large size and recent separation from the Malaysian peninsula all helped to preserve the diversity of its fauna. Until 100 years ago, Sumatra was still mostly forested. True, there were extensive areas of agriculture in the highlands of North and Western Sumatra, but except for these and the settlements along the coasts and rivers, the hinterlands remained much as they had been for thousands of years.

With the introduction of the plantation industries, accelerating population growth and the intensification of logging, the equation changed. Today, the forests of Sumatra appear to be a string of islands in a sea of modified land. Some of these "islands" are still extensive, however, and one of the most pristine is the wilderness that extends through the central regions of Aceh province. Some parts of this region are so remote they rarely feel the tread of man.

My story begins here, for it was in this virgin land that I first experienced the beauty of Sumatra's rainforests.

"*Assalamualaikum,*" I called toward the hut that stood on stilts at the end of the steep path.

"*Wa'alaikum salam,*" voices chorused from inside the bark walls.

A door opened and I was welcomed in to the house of Alamshah, the master hunter.

I had met him two months before while carrying out a survey of tiger populations in southern Aceh. At that time, I had been so impressed by the man's exceptional knowledge of the forest that I proposed we do a trip together. Despite suffering from acute tuberculosis, he agreed.

"The best time is toward the end of the dry season," he had said. "If we are lucky we may even see a rhino." Such a thought was tantalizing, for Sumatran rhinos were already very rare and few people ever had the chance of seeing them.

Now I was back and preparations were in full swing for the upcoming trip. Alamshah's wife was sorting through a sack full of rice, scooping a few handfuls into a woven tray and dexterously tossing the grains to separate any fine dirt and husks. A daughter, the eldest of seven children, roasted coffee in a *kuali* (a round-bottomed frying pan) over an open fire, then pounded the beans in a hollowed-out block of wood, using a hardwood pestle that was taller than she was. The coffee turned out to be excellent.

The men who were to carry the loads were repairing their packs—tall basket-like affairs made of rattan. One of the men had taken a long strip of bark from the *tarok* tree and after beating and washing it to void the sap, he was fashioning the tough fibrous material into head and shoulder straps.

That night, by the light of small kerosene lamps, Alamshah entertained me with hunting stories while his wife chopped up betel nut for him and suckled her youngest child. He spoke of a place high in the mountains where the clouds were ever present and the stunted trees were covered in thick layers of moss. He and his friends had spent a night there but they were too cold to sleep and in the morning they planned on setting off down to the lowlands. Instead, within a few hundred meters they came face to face with a rhino.

"There was a cloud of small sandflies around the rhino and we were bitten, so we must have been close," Alamshah said.

Since there were no strong trees to climb, the two parties just looked at each other and waited. Finally the rhino snorted and bolted off down the ridge.

"How many times have you seen rhino?" I asked.

Alamshah thought briefly. "In 25 years, just seven times."

If rhinos were so rarely seen when they were still relatively common, what hope was there now that they were truly rare? Not much, I decided, and fell asleep to dream of forests and mountains.

A cock crowing somewhere beneath the floorboards of the hut woke me in the early hours. It was still dark but the women were already up, preparing food in the "kitchen," just a sand hearth in one corner of the hut. The women in this part of Aceh work very hard, taking care not only of the home and children but also spending long hours each day in the rice fields. Their men are frequently away for long periods and so they learn to be very responsible. The amazing thing is that they seem to be so happy.

The men arrived at first light and divided the loads between them. Rice, dried fish, chilies, onions, salt, sugar and coffee was the simple list of food supplies and a diet to which I would grow accustomed in the years ahead. Two sheets of black plastic, some *tikar* (sleeping mats) woven from pandanus leaves, and a *parang* (machete) for each man completed the list of essential items.

Alamshah's house was situated in southern Aceh. Directly behind his simple abode and extending north for 150 kilometers was an unbroken tract of virgin rainforest, much of it mountainous. In the southern part there were still great expanses of lowland forest, the richest of all the many forest types in North Sumatra.

After a final smoke, and for Alamshah a slice of betel nut, we put on our packs and set off.

Frequently the word "impenetrable" is used to describe the rainforest. Perhaps this is because most people see only the forest's edge, where there is usually a zone of dense new growth. But by viewing the forest from inside, one gains a totally new perspective. Like a great cathedral or mosque, the interior is dominated by tall columns, the trunks of the largest of the forest trees. Their bases are commonly surrounded by radiating buttresses that help stabilize the tree, whose trunk might rise clearly 30 meters to the lowest branches and support a crown as high as that again. In the forests of southern Aceh the most important trees are the *damar*, a source of resin that oozes from wounds on the trunk; the *meranti*, with its brown, vertically striated bark, a wood considered to be the equivalent of mahogany; *simantuk*, with timber even more valuable; *krueng*, a tree that yields a fine oil; *kapur*, the source of camphor and weather-resistant timber; and *tualang*, the king of trees, soaring above all others and reaching heights of over 80 meters. *Tualang* is too hard to be a commercial timber and so it is frequently left standing after all other trees are cut down. Its clean white bark makes it difficult for bears to climb, and bees often build their lobate nests on the underside of its branches.

The columnar trunks of these and many other trees support the canopy, the leafy roof of the forest that is the dwelling place of monkeys, apes, birds, squirrels, certain snakes and a host of insects. Here, the greatest of Asia's apes, the red-haired orang-utan, forages for fruits, leaves and insects. Epiphytes and orchids find a home, and one of the tallest of forest trees, the giant fig, begins life here as a seedling. After first sending down fine roots to the ground, the fig's branches grow rapidly. Further roots wrap around the trunk, forming an ever-thickening network and supporting vigorous growth of foliage above. Ultimately, the host dies and the fig supports itself on an intricate framework of roots that mirror in form the trunk of the original tree. This largest of the world's parasites provides fruit in abundance, and without these trees many of the animals of the forest might die out.

Between the tree trunks, in the shade beneath the canopy, is a twilight world of lesser trees, saplings, seedlings, rattans, ferns and bamboos. Woody vines that hang from the large trees almost reach ground level, adding sweeping lines to a world dominated by verticals. But one's general impression is of relative openness of 50 to 100 meters in any direction.

The forest floor is home to the large mammals such as the elephant, rhino, tiger, rusa deer and *kijang* (barking deer) —although one rarely sees them. All these animals have acute hearing and most also have sensitive noses, and after long contact with man they have learned to be wary.

What one does see, however, are the insects. In my opinion, ants must be the rulers of the forest. From the forest floor to the tops of the trees I have seen their disciplined columns and scattered groups everywhere. From three centimeters long to almost invisible, they work by day or night and can drive one to distraction. Several times during that first trip we were forced out of camp when ants invaded us. One night we decided to fight back. The ants had probably massed around our camp in the early evening but we never noticed them until we received our first painful bites around 9 p.m. Lifting up our sleeping mats, we found the ground teeming with ants, so we spread hot embers and ash all over the ground to drive them out. As their confused squadrons reassembled, we encircled the camp with fires of burning amber, and secure within this ring of spitting flames and resinous smoke, we were able to sleep without further intrusions.

Most ants are benign enough so that when they are disturbed, their best defense is to run off. But a blue-gray solitary ant squirts a small mist of fluid when it is alarmed. The fluid smells of aniseed, and if it comes in contact with the skin, the pleasant odor lasts for up to an hour.

Whereas ants are occasionally a nuisance, other insects delight the senses. When a shaft of sunlight penetrates the labyrinth of foliage and strikes a patch of damp sand, it frequently reveals colorful carpets of butterflies. Dragonflies and damselflies hover near streams, and particularly where the sun is bright, their iridescence shows off to maximum advantage. Bees too are abundant, some smaller than house flies and others twice the size of the common honey bee. Honey bees build hives that hang either from the limbs of trees or from limestone cliffs, where they are safe from marauding bears.

Reptiles, though abundant, are rarely visible. Snakes are actually excellent camouflage artists and often a person can pass close to one without realizing it. Chameleons have even greater powers of camouflage, and although tortoises and turtles don't need to disguise themselves their colors blend in well with the background.

Most often it is the sounds that alert one to the presence of forest animals: the singing of the gibbons and siamangs, the goose-like honking of hornbills, the piercing wolf whistle of the argus pheasant, the roar of an agitated barking deer, and the monotonous buzzing of insects. Hearing these sounds became like seeing familiar faces, and collectively they meant that the forest was alive and well. Lesser creatures too—small birds, frogs, various cicadas and many other insects—all have their calling hours that mark the passage of time in the forest.

On the third day of that first trip we reached a *senong*, a mineral spring. Such springs or seepages are magnets for wildlife, particularly for the larger mammals, which come from far away to drink the mineral-rich water. *Senong* are scattered throughout the forest, but this one was special because of its size—about $\frac{1}{2}$ hectare of damp silt.

When we arrived, we found tracks of elephant, rhino, rusa deer, barking deer, tiger, clouded leopard and many smaller creatures—clear evidence that this was prime rainforest. Alamshah had seen rhino here in the past, and he told of one occasion when he had approached this place and found the entire *senong* filled with countless deer milling around in circles, as if fenced in. The deer were so preoccupied that they never became aware of the silent observers who sat fascinated for almost an hour.

According to old hunters, *senongs* are the abodes of spirits that guard the welfare of the animals, and so it was forbidden to set traps within 200 meters of a *senong*. Alamshah himself considered such places important in the life cycles of the large animals, particularly the rhino, which he suspected sometimes met others of its own kind there.

The *senong* we saw was located near the Air Putih river, a distant tributary to the Bengkung, which itself flows into the Alas river, one of the main waterways of Aceh. For much of its length, the Air Putih flows through flat or gently undulating land, a large plain really, that is almost completely surrounded by hills. In those days (just four years ago) it was all forested, for the hills formed a barrier and few people ventured there.

In the remaining 10 days of our trip we wandered widely through these forests, soaking up the sights, smells and sounds of this world. And a new world it was, for instead of being the hothouse, fever-ridden hells of old accounts, these forests were cool and fresh, the streams were clear and we could drink from them without ill effect. Mosquitos were almost totally absent and leeches at this time of year were not a great problem either.

*An aerial view of a rainforest in central Aceh.*

*Overleaf: In the mountains of central Aceh.*

The streams abounded with various fish, crabs and prawns.

I also began to recognize the subtle signs of animals—the smear of mud on a tree from a passing deer or pig, a creased leaf from a sharp hoof, the milky water in a recently used wallow, the telltale sheer patterns on a severed stalk indicating which animal had eaten there, and much more.

These were, however, just signs. It was the animals themselves that I really wanted to see and record, and my mind was already working on ideas. Alamshah felt that at least for rhinos and elephants, long and careful stalking would bring rewards.

I felt this would be impossible in view of his worsening health. During the night, his coughing fits went on for hours. He often ran fevers and his body was wasted. He was a determined man, however, and after a particularly bad bout of coughing he offered me a deal: "Cure me of this disease, Boss, and I will guide you through these forests for as long as you want." I had no idea what the future held but we shook hands anyway.

Two months later, after starting Alamshah on medication, we were back in the forest. But that expedition ended in disaster. A log on which Alamshah and I had been resting broke, and in the ensuing fall my parang cut deeply into Alamshah's foot. It took five days to carry him out and I felt certain he would never walk properly again.

*Below: The humid forest at dawn. Right: Typical view from inside the forest. The stream, though small, is rich in fish.*

*The fungi of the rainforest display an extraordinary diversity
in shape and color.*

*Below: Durian is a fruit with a strong smell that attracts animals from great distances to feed on them.*
*Left: The asam is another fruit that enriches the jungle diet.*

*Some ants' nests (left) display highly complex structures, whereas beehives are simple in form. Overleaf: Although they normally nest on the underside of tree limbs, bees also seek sanctuary on cliffs.*

*Two masters of camouflage: A toad and a butterfly.*

*Right: Although many spiders roam freely through the forest for their prey, this one has built a web and devours a grasshopper.*

*Below: Damselflies haunt the waterways of the forest, where their insect prey abounds.*

*Left and below: Striking examples of warning coloration. Both these insects inflict great pain to anyone who accidentally steps on them.*

*Chameleons are among the most attractive lizards—and much sought after by tree snakes (overleaf).*

*Left: The squirrel is one of the few commonly seen mammals in the forest. Right: Skinks with forked tails are rare and much prized, since the Acehnese believe they can bring good luck for the next rice crop.*

Overleaf: A mangrove snake feeding on a chameleon.

A year would elapse before I returned to the Air Putih. At the time I had other commitments, and Alamshah's health was not up to extended treks. Miraculously, after a doctor treated his wounded foot in Medan, it began to heal and in three months he was walking well again.

Meanwhile, during my spare time, I set to work investigating techniques for capturing forest animals on film. Wildlife photography is rather like hunting in that you can shoot or trap. Having seen so few animals during my first two expeditions, I decided that shooting had a low chance of success, so I went ahead and made some initial attempts at the photographic equivalent of trapping—that is, the use of automatically triggered cameras. The principle is simple enough: A camera is set up at a promising location, where a passing animal triggers a pressure switch or photoelectric device, which fires the camera. These techniques have been used elsewhere and they have the advantage of maintaining around-the-clock surveillance of an area. So I worked on the real problem of making the devices operational in a rainforest environment.

On weekends too I traveled to southern Aceh to learn more about the animals there and to check on Alamshah and the men. When Alamshah could walk again, he suggested that we perform a purification ceremony. "It's like this, Boss. It wasn't your fault that my foot was wounded. It was a sign from those that govern the forest that we dared enter and work there without introducing ourselves correctly. The spirits had given other signs to turn back but I ignored them and I suffered this accident for my arrogance." Alamshah had expressed similar sentiments soon after the accident and I marveled at a culture that could so cleverly displace the blame from the real perpetrator (myself) and thus preserve the unity and harmony of our small group.

So I agreed, and in a few days the chattering of women and laughter of children rang around Alamshah's house as coconuts were grated, chickens slaughtered and rice cooked in preparation for the purification ritual or *selamatan*. The men inside smoked, ate betel nut and talked.

Around midday, two Muslim elders arrived. After the usual introductions they went into the sleeping quarters of the house, together with Alamshah's mother-in-law (a woman of considerable learning) and all of us who had taken part in the ill-fated expedition. There, we were served a tray of ceremonial food, in the center of which was a large cake of sticky rice shaped like an inverted bowl, topped by the relief of a flower made of ginger and sugar. Around the cake in small dishes were yellow rice, a green paste and a bunch of sirih leaves beside a bowl of scented water. Prayers were offered. The mother-in-law then dropped some yellow rice over our heads and hands, and used the sirih leaves to lightly sprinkle water over each of us. She smeared green paste behind our ears. Our jungle knives received the treatment as well, and when she had finished, the two elders repeated the ceremony. Now that we were purified, we relaxed and the feasting began.

Only a week after this episode, the durian fruit in the orchards that bordered the nearby forest began to ripen and fall. Some of these orchards are commonly owned, so anyone from the village can collect as much fruit as he pleases. At the height of the season there is a holiday atmosphere as small groups of men leave their houses in the evening to seek out favorite trees and pass the night sitting, talking and waiting for the football-sized fruit to fall—which they do with a loud thud that can be heard from some distance away. No one gets much chance to sleep, since most durians seem to fall at night, and particularly in the early hours of the morning.

I had just arrived in the village when two of my men, Sukiman and Samsul, mentioned they were going to collect durians and offered to take me along. Since I was tired from a long drive, I declined—and have regretted it ever since.

Later that night Samsul was searching for a durian that had just fallen when he noticed that a tiger had beaten him to the prize. Tigers apparently love durians (as do bears, orang-utans and elephants), so Samsul retreated to join Sukiman and another friend on a bare patch of ground about 20 meters away. There, the three of them sat back-to-back in fear as the tiger opened the spiky fruit with his claws, then removed seeds one by one to lick off the surrounding pulp, dropping the cleaned seeds in a neat pile nearby. Some experts doubt that a tiger will eat durian, and I wish I had been there to prove them wrong.

When I next had the opportunity to collect the fruit, I readily accepted. That day, although we saw no tigers, we did see one freshly opened fruit spread out like the petals of a flower, with the characteristic pile of cleanly licked seeds beside it.

By this time the remote cameras were ready for some field-testing, so I traveled to southern Aceh almost every weekend to check on them. On these trips I also studied the surprisingly abundant wildlife around the edge of the forest behind the villages. There, the numerous pigs find much food to their liking in the unfenced gardens, particularly cassava roots and *kemiri* nuts. Tigers made regular visits and their presence kept the pigs on the move. Later, when the tigers were poisoned, the damage to the rice fields increased dramatically. On this visit, I saw both fresh tiger prints and clouded leopard prints within 15 meters of the house I stayed in. Rusa deer could sometimes be heard calling at night with a curious bell-like bark, and porcupines maintained regular routes as they foraged in the darkness. Bats were common and some came to suck the nectar from the durian blossoms and, incidentally, pollinate this important fruit. We frequently saw snakes, including the king cobra, but the reputedly common

black cobra eluded me until the end. Being so close to the forest itself, we could hear the calls of siamang, gibbon, langurs and every so often a visiting orang-utan. Hornbills were ever present and their croaking, honking calls are one of the most evocative sounds of the rainforest.

From time to time I visited the swamp forests that extended from nearby to the coast 20 kilometers away. These are the kind of environments many people identify with rainforests: constantly wet, huge trees with great buttressed roots, mosquitoes day and night, pythons and other snakes, semi-aquatic tigers—and crippling diseases such as malaria and elephantiasis.

Here, one can still find crocodiles and soft-shelled, fresh-water turtles so heavy it requires four men to lift them from the water. For a long time few people ventured into such areas, for fear that they harbored dangerous spirits. But the demand for timber, rattan and fish has overcome such fears, and gradually people are moving in. These forests also support great concentrations of birds and, near the coast, flocks of pigeons and parrots appear at dusk in great clouds to settle in secure roosting places.

The rainforest proved a much tougher environment for using the remote cameras than I had expected. Termites and ants ate through the electrical leads, rats gnawed some of the hardware, moisture from the rain and humidity played havoc with the electronics and caused fungus to build up on the lenses. Even tigers added to the carnage, sometimes by crushing batteries and once by puncturing a camera.

Often, some small thing would malfunction and the result would be yet another roll of darkness. Each failure, however, pointed the way to success and after many months of tests, the men and I felt confident enough to take the cameras several days' walk into the forest.

Some of the subsequent results were more encouraging and for the first time I was able to get a glimpse at the life that was hidden in the forest.

A series of photos of some Asian wild dogs marked a turning point, primarily because in the rainforest environment it would have been virtually impossible to photograph these rare animals in any other way. The photos also confirmed that the techniques we had painstakingly developed were now sufficiently advanced to encourage further work. Perhaps most significant though was that four months after I took the photographs, the very same dogs died when feeding off a poisoned bait laid out for tigers. Time was running out for some of the rarer animals and the urgency for recording them was forever intensifying.

*Below: The long muzzle of this shrew-faced ground squirrel reflects the carniverous diet that distinguishes it from its tree-dwelling ancestors. Right: Despite its long spines, the porcupine is often preyed upon by tigers.*

*Left: The diminutive mouse deer is especially common near the forest's edge.*

*Below: A Malayan wood rat feeding on an earthworm.*

*Above: The python, a non-venomous snake especially common in swampy areas. Right: Despite its colorful markings, the crested fireback is seldom seen.*

*Pigeons are common in the lowlands of south Aceh and display a great range of colorful plumage.*
*Overleaf: Though crocodiles are now rare in Sumatra, a few still inhabit the rivers of southwestern Aceh.*

# Elephants

Shortly after our initial success with the remote cameras, Mobil Oil Indonesia generously provided funding necessary to sustain a long-term commitment to record a broad cross section of rainforest life. One of my first priorities was to reestablish contact with an elephant herd that lived in the forested foothills inland from Mobil's Arun gas field in north Aceh.

The elephant and its prehistoric cousins, the mastodons and mammoths, once roamed from Europe to China, Siberia to India, Africa to Timor, and throughout the Americas. In fact, they thrived until early man unleashed his hunting skills on these biggest of land mammals. Gradually their numbers declined and today they are found only in Africa, India and South East Asia.

The elephants that live in Sumatra belong to the Asian species *Elephas maximus*. They are not as big as the African variety and instead of having the graceful swayed back of their African cousins, the Asian elephants are either humped or straight backed. Their ears are not as large either and remind me of a piece of tattered, dirty cloth hanging from a pole. The tusks are smaller too and are almost always absent in the female. But Sumatran elephants are still imposing animals when seen at close quarters and their intelligence and willingness to be trained sometimes made them a great asset before this age of bulldozers and trucks. As many as 900 elephants served in the army of Aceh's great Sultan Iskandar Muda and until quite recently, elephants were used in the province as beasts of burden.

Elephants are the pathmakers of the forest. In their migrations they clear fallen trees from trails and create new routes to feeding grounds, and we were often able to capitalize on their work and make rapid progress through otherwise difficult country.

I like to think that elephants are caretakers as well. It seems that they must examine—and usually destroy—anything foreign to them. This applied particularly to our permanent camps, one of which was flattened three times by some elephants that seemed to take particular delight in ripping out the plastic sheeting from our roof and flattening our rice storage tins.

To observe these great pachyderms I went to north Aceh near the town of Lhokseumawe where several years before I had had my first encounters with Sumatran elephants.

At that time there was a herd of over 30 individuals which regularly visited a developing rubber estate and caused damage to the young rubber trees. By day, the herd remained in the forest that bordered the estate, and at dusk the elephants would emerge to feed not only on the young saplings that they would pluck from the ground in order to eat the roots, but also on a variety of leguminous plants specially planted for weed control.

On the first occasion, Sani, a foreman on the plantation, took us to a ridge with a view toward the forest where we expected the elephants to be residing. A small band of macaque monkeys crashed through the trees and a pair of hornbills honked, but otherwise there was silence. It wasn't until the sunlight had disappeared from the tops of the trees that we heard a sharp trumpet-like blast from within the forest. Ten minutes later there was another, followed by the sound of breaking branches as the animals began to forage closer to the forest's edge.

Looking into the forest, I could see the top of a tree swaying wildly as an elephant—or elephants—tried to pull it down to get at the uppermost foliage. I was so engrossed in this display of raw elephant power that I missed seeing a trunk emerge from the dense wall of growth at the forest's edge.

The trunk was raised and waving to the left and right, testing the air. Satisfied that there was no immediate danger, its owner followed—a full-grown cow elephant. Others followed silently, their bodies muddy from having wallowed earlier in the day and their backs covered with leaves and other debris. Among the cows were young ones and even one infant, closely surrounded by three matrons. Last to appear, some distance behind the others, was a bull. He had only one tusk. The other one may have been broken in a fight, for Sani claimed the animal was truculent.

By reputation, elephants are quiet and at times they certainly can be, but when a herd is feeding contentedly it produces a whole symphony of sounds. Apart from tearing up saplings, breaking branches and chewing fibrous food, there was a steady accompaniment of snorts, belches and whistling of air through their trunks, as well as stomach rumbles and the odd squeak and trumpet blast.

The animals in this herd had become accustomed to humans, so they approached fairly close to us. I discovered that elephants have a characteristic smell, a not unpleasant mixture of horse and honey. In the future, that smell would often alert me to elephants.

The herd actually covered a large territory that was centered on the Pase river but extended as far as the Kertau river in the south and was bounded on the north by mountains and to the east by settlement.

When I returned in 1986 with the intention of following the herd for longer periods, my companion was Pak Yusuf from the forestry headquarters in Lhokseumawe. Yusuf was unusually valuable in his willingness to follow the elephants he knew so well. At times, though, Yusuf's courage verged on recklessness, as he frequently approached to within 10 meters of the animals.

Off and on we would return to see the herd, sometimes just for a few days but more often for extended periods. We followed the animals by day, lived off very skimpy rations and slept near where the herd fed after nightfall.

One of our first encounters occurred on the middle reaches of the Pase river, which at that time was completely surrounded by forest. We had taken up temporary residence in an abandoned hut about half a kilometer downstream from a fording place regularly used by the herd. Just upstream was a large, deep pool at the turn of the river—a favorite bathing place for the herd.

Late in the afternoon Yusuf and I carefully approached the ford and hid among the boulders and grass of the river bank. We had a hunch that the herd might soon emerge from the forest.

Two hours later, we were about to decide our hunch had been wrong when the first cow elephant appeared. She tested the air and to our amazement began crossing the river. Although she soon got wind of our scent, she apparently decided we were not a threat and joined three others who were feeding in the scrub that bordered the river banks.

A second group then appeared, and a single cow approached the pool. At the edge of the beach, she turned around and cautiously backed into the river. When she was almost submerged, the others followed, headfirst. Soon there were 18 animals in that pool, including infants. Others remained on the beach and down the opposite bank. It appeared that the pool was surrounded by cows acting as sentries. I have, in fact, noticed this same drill on other occasions as well.

Suddenly something alarmed the cow nearest us and she trumpeted one clear blast. Within seconds, all the elephants were out of the water and standing motionless on the beach. After several minutes, the juveniles as a group ran into the water, splashing and squealing like children. The adults followed and again the pool was filled with shining black heads and snorkel-like trunks. The water bubbled, and over the surface rose clouds of spray as the great beasts blew water into the air and over their backs.

Bathing seemed to be so much fun that it was surprising that those cows still on the beach did not join in. In studying them, I noticed for the first time the most magnificent bull I had yet seen. His body was tall but very heavily muscled, and his tusks were long and curved like bows. He just stood there at the forest's edge swinging his trunk slowly and moving his weight from one foot to another. Darkness came quickly and with it the images of the elephants disappeared. In the months that followed, I began to wonder if the dim light had been playing tricks with me and if somehow my imagination had exaggerated what my eyes saw; even worse, I feared that the bull had been shot for the ivory he bore. Although we frequently followed the herd, I saw nothing like that great bull who had appeared so majestically that evening beside the Pase. He had vanished as surely as if he had never been.

By following the herd for days on end, we began to learn their ways and even, sometimes, to predict their movements correctly. On one particularly memorable day, the weather had held and we had followed the animals all morning through some particularly dense forest. Later in the afternoon I expected the herd to emerge on a dirt road near the boundary of a new rubber estate. The sun would be in the right direction, the light in the open area would allow shutter speeds fast enough to freeze the action, and the forest behind would form the perfect backdrop.

As expected, the elephants began to emerge from the undergrowth—single females first, followed by a sub-adult male. I was hidden on a small knoll opposite them and was waiting for more of them to appear when a plantation truck came by—the only vehicle all day. As the men on the back of the truck shouted and the driver stopped and honked his horn, the elephants retreated. I had almost given up hope of photographing them when Yusuf persuaded the men to move on.

The elephants, however, did not retreat far and half an hour later they appeared from the same patch of forest. But again I was robbed of the chance of getting any good shots, because just then a man rode up on his motorbike. He was the chief of the nearby village of Uram Jalan, who had once been an elephant hunter. This time Yusuf's powers of persuasion failed. After all, a chief wasn't going to be told what to do, especially when he wanted to show that he wasn't afraid of the elephants. He started up his motorbike again while the elephants retreated down the road and I came out of my hiding spot.

I explained to the chief what I had been doing. "You can easily overtake them," he said, offering to show me how. This was the last thing I needed, but out of desperation I set off to skirt the side of the valley along which the road ran. Using what cover I could, I tried to get ahead of the elephants; no luck, they just walked faster and then moved down into a forested ravine running parallel to the road. The faster I ran, the faster the elephants moved. Now all the herd was in the ravine, racing along, kicking up dust and making the ground rumble with the tramping of their feet. As they approached the narrowest part of the ravine, I left my camera and tripod and ran for all I was worth. Somehow the elephants knew I was there and stampeded, crashing through the bush with reckless speed as they passed through the bottleneck and out toward the village of Uram Jalan.

Completely by myself and quite unintentionally, I had driven a herd of over 20 elephants through a small gorge. In fact I had accidentally rediscovered a prehistoric hunting technique, for if a trap had been set at the bottom of that ravine, the entire herd could have been eliminated. It had all been so easy. No wonder the big game of Europe, Asia and America was decimated by those early hunters.

While following the Pase herd and also in the great forests to the south, I noticed how the presence of elephants seems to draw other animals to the same locations. Many times after elephants had passed through a certain area, we saw the tracks of other animals—such as rusa, barking deer, pig and civet cat—where none had been for months before. I don't know why this is so, though in the case of tigers there is perhaps one explanation.

As elephants move through the forest and feed, they disturb animals residing there that might provide easy meals for a resourceful tiger. On several occasions I have seen tigers near elephant herds—one time only 300 meters away—and the elephants never showed alarm, so presumably it is not unusual.

If, however, a tiger suddenly passes by and surprises the herd, the result is a cacophony of trumpeting and screaming as almost all the members join in. Perhaps the elephants are concerned for the infants, since a tiger is presumably quite capable of bringing one down, but from my observations the youngest members of the herd are so well guarded that it would be a risky undertaking for the tiger.

Even when crossing a path or open space, the adults show the same protective care. Single females go first, then an "aunt" will stand in the open space while the mother and infant pass by on the safe side.

I have seen the elephants show the same protection when they are resting. One morning after a night of heavy rain, the Pase herd rested up on a grassy river bank. It is unusual for Sumatran elephants to rest in the open, but perhaps because it was cool and the neighboring forest flooded, the river bank seemed the best place for them.

Whatever the reasons for their choice, the elephants arranged themselves so that eight cows lay along the edge of the river bank just two meters above the water. The remaining adults placed themselves along the boundary of the forest, facing toward it and standing virtually motionless except for the flapping of their ears. In this way the animals had formed a circle, in the middle of which was a bundle of young ones sleeping, dozing and sometimes playing. This scene lasted from 10 a.m. to 1 p.m. and was only disrupted when some woodcutters came upon the herd and shouted to drive the elephants away.

Because of the pressure for land in the Pase valley, there was increasing conflict between the elephants and man. One evening just after dark the herd emerged from some forest that bordered the river to travel to a feeding ground in another tract of forest, a few kilometers away to the north. In the process, however, they had to pass through a valley where a few dozen families had established gardens. It had happened before, and this time the settlers were prepared.

When I arrived at the scene, the valley was filled with fires that had been lit to drive the elephants back and to protect the houses and gardens. People were screaming, some out of fear, but most in attempts to drive the elephants away. Arcs of flame cut through the darkness as rags soaked in kerosene were ignited and hurled at the animals. Nearby, elephants screamed out of fear of fire. Carbide cannons (long pipes in which carbide and water are mixed and the resulting methane is ignited) were set off with deafening

effect. The atmosphere was reminiscent of a battle in full fury.

Amazingly, most of the elephants ran the gauntlet and some stragglers even remained on the upper end of the valley feeding on young banana trees. When Yusuf was asked to chase the animals away, he was in a squeeze because it was his job to protect both the elephant herd and the welfare of the settlers. So in a deft act of diplomacy he walked right up to the elephants and shouted at them in Acehnese to go home to a tributary of the Pase where at that time no settlements had been established. The settlers were more impressed than the elephants. In the early hours of the morning, however, the elephants caused more problems when some of them discovered a pile of durians—a fruit they are extremely fond of.

Ultimately, the herd became an intolerable nuisance and some experts were brought in to capture the elephants. For me and Yusuf, it was sad to think that the elephants we had now been observing off and on for over a year were to lose their wild freedom, so we decided to see them one more time. We caught up with the herd on a high ridge overlooking the Pase river and by late afternoon began our approach.

We were confronted by the usual sounds—breaking branches and the snapping of giant bamboo that sounded like a volley of rifle fire. We directed our search to where the noise was greatest, taking care to avoid any stragglers. Closing in slowly, we could make out the stone-colored shapes of two or three elephants. I set up the camera and took time out to observe more closely. Through the tangled and dry understory I could now see one elephant less than 15 meters away that had an extraordinary set of tusks—the largest I'd seen in a long time. His body was fully fleshed and his head had a high bulge on top. Something must have alerted him, for he swiveled around and looked right at me. In that instant I knew it was the bull I had seen so long ago at the bathing pool on the Pase.

He sniffed the air with raised trunk and seemed to detect nothing. Still agitated, he let the top of his trunk touch the ground to suck up dirt and leaves, and defiantly blew the stuff over his back. He repeated this several times before someone moved and he spun around again, to charge and crash away through the undergrowth.

That was the last time I saw that great herd. Afterward I vowed to look for elephants that lived in areas still unaffected by man, where they could go about their business unharried. Actually it was the elephants that took the initiative, as I learned when Alamshah arrived at my house after one of his trips into the forest to change film in the remote cameras.

"How did it go?" I asked.

"No good, Boss. Some elephants destroyed your cameras."

Alamshah was never one for disguising the facts. He handed me two plastic bags full of alloy pieces, twisted electrical circuits, solenoids and broken glass.

"We couldn't find all the pieces. They were spread over a wide area and had been trodden into the ground."

It appeared that a lone elephant had passed by two of our camera locations, and upon detecting the cameras, decided to investigate. First he plucked the cameras off their mountings, then chewed them to pieces.

So began our relationship with a herd of elephants that inhabited an area of lowland forest below the southern boundary of Gunung Leser National Park.

The place where the cameras had been installed is roughly at the center of the herd's natural range and is very important for all wildlife, as it forms a corridor between two extensive tracts of forest otherwise separated by a gorge almost 1,000 meters deep. There, the soil is rich, growth of vegetation fast, and water abundant. The trails in some places here are so well worn that they look like miniature avenues and it would be easy to ride a motorbike along some stretches. I named the place "*Rambung*" after the fig trees that were abundant there.

In the undisturbed state, elephants constantly migrate through large territories, and appear at certain key parts of the range with surprising regularity, varying by only a few days from year to year. Perhaps I should have considered these things when I passed through *Rambung* almost exactly a year after those first two cameras had been destroyed.

Gadi, one of my strongest assistants, was traveling with me at the time and the two of us were making good progress in the cool morning air. As we walked we could see abundant signs that elephants had been there—toppled plantains, masticated vines, fresh droppings and several sets of tracks. One set was headed in the same direction we were going, so I readied my camera in anticipation. As I did so, I explained to Gadi how it is quite possible to pass by an elephant and never even know he is there. An elephant can stand perfectly still for long periods (I timed one for 14 minutes) and when it does so, its earth-colored body looks like just another part of the forest.

Barely five minutes after giving this little dissertation, I walked right by the elephant whose tracks we had been following. I would never have realized his existence had he not exhaled air through his trunk with that characteristic windy sound ending in a low rumble. The sound arrested me. I spun around to find myself looking right between a set of tusks into the face of a mighty bull elephant barely four meters away. I expected he would turn and run, but this bull was in "musth" (mating condition) and had no such idea. Instead, he came straight for me, tusks raised and ears out.

In the short time it takes an elephant to cover four meters, I

was able to run to safety among the lattice work of aerial roots of a giant fig tree, which by the grace of the spirits of that forest was only a short distance away. We both reached the tree about the same time and when I looked around from the safety of my tangled fortress, all I could see was a huge mass of brown and a trunk trying to penetrate the network of roots. The sweet smell of elephant that I had earlier failed to detect now filled my nostrils. The heavy exhalation of air and the sound of that great body rubbing against the roots dominated my troubled senses. Eventually, however, he moved on up the trail, perhaps frustrated or more likely repelled by the smell of a human being.

I emerged to find Gadi 20 meters back, standing beside his pack, which he had placed on the ground in anticipation of escape. He smiled, and admitted he had been frightened, but to his credit he was still willing to carry on and follow the elephant. Though we never saw the elephant again, by taking note of his tracks we established a remote camera nearby and eventually captured him on film.

*A herd of elephants feeding on the fringes of a newly developed rubber plantation. Overleaf: When the wind is right and no sounds intrude, an elephant may come quite close before detecting a human's presence.*

*Left: A young siamang swinging back to its mother.*
*Below: From high up in a fig tree, a gibbon spots the photographer.*

*Below and right: Two long-tailed macaques—one surveying its group from an elevated log, the other walking along the branch of a fig tree in search of food.*

*Left: The largest bull elephant the photographer saw in east Aceh. Below: Elephants bathing in the Pase river. Overleaf: A group feeding in the late afternoon. The elephant with the tusks will move apart from the herd once it reaches maturity.*

*Right: A remote camera captures the same elephant that charged the photographer almost a year earlier at this same place. Below: A young elephant barely 1.5 meters tall is followed by its mother.*

the morning when the male and female of a family group re-establish their territory. It is even better when several groups sing at the same time, each from its respective territory. Then the whole forest seems to ring with a mixture of sustained notes and staccato ones, and some vibrato-enriched glissandos.

The vocalizations of gibbons and siamangs are perhaps the most characteristic sounds of the Sumatran rainforests and rarely a day goes by without hearing them. Siamangs produce an even louder sound—a rich contralto voice—and the singing, really a duet of male and female, can carry up to two kilometers through the forest.

Siamangs are handsome animals; with the exception of their black faces, they are covered almost entirely with sleek black hair. Although they don't have the same degree of nervous energy as gibbons, they are still fine performers—and what they lack in speed, they make up in strength and grace.

Like the gibbon, the siamang eats many of the wild fruits that are available in the rainforest throughout most of the year, but because it derives a large percentage of its diet from young leaves it is also capable of living at higher altitudes.

Even in the treetops, the gibbons and siamangs pick up irritating nits and insects in their fur. So on most days the animals spend up to an hour grooming each other. Judging by the languid posture of a siamang stretched out along a branch 60 meters above the ground with three of his limbs hanging limply down and eyes half closed, I can only assume that being groomed is a highly pleasurable and relaxing experience. Since each member of a group has its turn, the exercise may go beyond mere delousing and perhaps enhance the harmony of the family.

In the late afternoon gibbons and siamangs begin to search for a place to spend the night. Unlike the orang-utan, which builds a nest and has little to fear from predators, the two smaller relatives must do with a fork in a tree. But not just any tree will do. A tree that is fruiting, for instance, might attract too many nocturnal visitors to allow a peaceful sleep; a tree that is too low might offer dangerous exposure to predators; and some trees, such as the wild figs, are frequently the abode of snakes. The number of trees in a given territory that meet the exacting requirements of gibbons or siamangs are few—far fewer than the number of days in a year—so the "sleeping" trees are like familiar campsites, to be returned to when the situation dictates.

High up in the branches, then, these agile primates settle down and await nightfall. One evening from a steep ridge I looked down on a sleeping tree and saw a gibbon reclining on his high perch. The wind was blowing and the branches swayed in a complicated pattern—enough, I'm sure, to make me seasick had I been there—but my little companion down below just turned over from time to time, at ease with his world as he waited for darkness

or sleep to overtake him.

All three of these animals are purists in the sense that they live in the tall forest and have not compromised their lifestyles in any way to suit man. Macaques, on the other hand, have not only adapted to man's presence but have openly exploited him.

In Sumatra, there are two species of macaques, the long-tailed and the pig-tailed. The long-tailed macaques can live in mangrove forests and throughout the lowlands, though they never seem to venture far from water. Their diet varies from crabs and aquatic algae to fruits and seeds. With such catholic taste they can easily be maintained in captivity and some live semi-wild around Hindu temples in Bali and India. The pig-tailed macaque is a larger animal and the males can reach a height of over 50 centimeters at the shoulder and sport a lion-like mane around the head and neck. They seem to spend much of their time on the ground, and of all the animals I photographed, these most commonly triggered my cameras. In the forest they cover a large territory—perhaps as much as 10 square kilometers—but around the villages they can live close to the gardens that they raid for corn, beans and bananas. For this, they are poisoned mercilessly.

Of the leaf monkeys, or langurs, Sumatra has many different types, all displaying different coloring from pure charcoal gray to rusty red. The ones that dominate in Aceh province, the Thomas leaf monkeys, are very dapper in appearance, having a dark gray back and white belly and underparts, a white face and black hair swept up into a central ridge. Primarily arboreal, these attractive animals forage for leaves and fruit in groups of seven to nine. Instead of brachiating as apes do, they walk, run and leap through the branches.

Finally, there is another primate that looks more like a miniature bear than a monkey. It is nocturnal and rarely seen, sleeping high up in the crowns of trees during the day and foraging slowly through the canopy at night, living it seems mainly on insects. It is the slow loris.

Once when watching an orang-utan move through the trees, I heard what I thought was a piece of dead wood fall to ground beside me. Feeling lucky that I wasn't hit, I went over to investigate and there discovered instead a small brown bundle of fur. It was a loris. Though stunned, it soon got up and waddled slowly to the nearest sapling, where it again climbed up into the canopy. I was amazed at the resilience of this mysterious creature.

It would have been a pleasure to spend a lot more time photographing primates. Active mostly in the canopy, they constitute a challenge, because they are difficult subjects to record faithfully on film. At the same time, they are fascinating to observe. I regretfully turned my attention from them to the terrestrial animals that for so long had eluded my best efforts and which I now sought in areas far from the influence of man.

*Left: The bond between a mother orang-utan and its child is a close and long one, lasting several years.*
*The color of orang-utans varies from rusty orange to the maroon of the male shown below.*

*Left: The bond between a mother orang-utan and its child is a close and long one, lasting several years.*
*The color of orang-utans varies from rusty orange to the maroon of the male shown below.*

The loss of cameras to some curious elephants interrupted my remote camera program, but in any case, the time had come to change direction.

For one thing, most of our remote stations were in forests that were now threatened. The great forests of the Air Putih, which only a year ago had been virtually free of humans, were now inundated with rattan collectors and settlers who were leveling the forest in order to plant crops. Logging companies were building roads into the area and had already started to cut timber on the perimeter. The Senong, where rhinos and elephants had once wallowed, was now surrounded by snares, and fishermen had poisoned the river with the pesticide endrin in order to increase their catch of fish for the markets in towns far away.

Clearly, we had to find new areas that were not only unspoiled but would remain so for the foreseeable future. So Alamshah began a series of surveys that would eventually take him into the heart of the Aceh wilderness.

In the meantime I began work on upgrading the camera systems to extend their life in the forest so that we could operate far from home without, for instance, having to change batteries so frequently.

When these problems were overcome I took the opportunity to make some trips to the Ketambe research station in Gunung Leuser National Park, where I was a guest of the park's researchers. It is not normal for outsiders to be welcomed there, since any interference can affect the behavior of the animals. But these hospitable scholars realized that my job would be made easier because many of the study groups had been somewhat habituated to man and might therefore offer opportunities for photography that were impossible elsewhere.

Sumatra is extraordinarily rich in primates, that diverse group of mammals that includes monkeys and apes. The Ketambe area alone has eight species, and perhaps the best known of all is the orang-utan. These engaging animals, and to a lesser degree, the white-handed gibbon and siamang, are considered to be closely related to man. For this reason, much research and observation have been directed at them in the hope that the knowledge gained might illuminate our own condition.

I have to admit that I lose my objectivity when I see these animals in the wild—a mother orang-utan tenderly stroking the head of the new-born infant she cradles in her arms, or a large male waking to find that it is raining and deciding he will procrastinate a little longer before getting up to look for food.

The orang-utans are the largest of Asia's apes, and are found only in Northern Sumatra and Borneo. Their shaggy, red-haired bodies are about the size of a man's, while the arms are longer and the legs shorter. When surprised, they can show remarkable bursts of energy and speed, but normally they move slowly, sit for

long periods and take an hour or so each day for a siesta. They are so quiet and calm that I must have passed beneath them many times without realizing it. Although they are probably aware of other orang-utans in the area, they are solitary. And because they are spaced so far apart, the male has developed a loud call to announce his whereabouts. When I first heard this call, it sounded like the repeated bellowing of a bull, rising quickly to full volume and then trailing away into a series of hooted grunts. The sound can carry for over a kilometer if the animals are on a ridge. Besides their deliberate calling, they will sometimes bellow on hearing a tree fall or a landslide, and some unscrupulous hunters stimulate the same call by hitting the buttress of a large tree with a heavy piece of wood to determine if orang-utans are in the area.

These red-haired creatures once inhabited the forests from India to China and throughout South East Asia, and it is puzzling why they should be found in so few places today. Certainly it is not for lack of ability to live in a variety of habitats, as I have seen them from sea-level swamp forests to altitudes as high as 1,700 meters. Neither is it due to a specialized diet, because orang-utans will feed off a wide variety of foods including fruit, bark, leaves, birds' eggs and insects. One large male, near where I was staying in the forests of southern Aceh, even raided some bee hives that hung from the branches of a huge *tualang* tree. On three successive days the orang-utan returned to gorge himself on the wild honey until he was satisfied—or was unable to stand the incessant swarming of bees around him.

Part of the reason for the orang-utans' decline may lie in the fact that man himself has hunted these peaceful animals and only where his impact has been slight does the orang-utan still survive.

The two relatives of the orang-utan, the gibbon and the siamang, are more specialized in their eating habits, living almost entirely off fruits and leaves. Of the two, the gibbon is the smaller and I have sometimes heard it referred to in Aceh as the clown monkey—presumably because its white "gloves" and almost mask-like black face remind some people of a clown. I like to think, however, that the real reason is that beneath its soft, beige-colored coat is the rugged body of an acrobat. And indeed, in the upper reaches of the trees, the gibbon is an undisputed master.

Gibbons normally move by brachiating—swinging hand over hand—and their speed and agility can be both breathtaking and beautiful. I spent half an hour once watching a young gibbon chase a leaf monkey (itself no mean performer) back and forth through the treetops for no other reason, as far as I could detect, than the sheer fun of it.

The usual Acehnese name for the gibbon is *Wut wut*, which is an approximation of one of the sounds they make. The approximation does not do justice to the clear soprano notes these animals can produce, and the best performances usually occur in

*Acehnese sometimes call the gibbon (left) "the clown monkey"*
*because of its white hands and white-ringed face.*
*Below: Grooming is an important social function for many*
*primates—as with this group of long-tailed macaques.*

*Leaf monkeys—or langurs—normally live in tree tops and show great caution whenever they are on the ground.*

*Below: The silvered leaf monkey prefers swamps and lowlands for its habitat. Right: The slow loris is the only nocturnal primate in Aceh.*

Through his surveys, Alamshah had found areas in the remotest parts of the Aceh wilderness that seemed promising for our work. He described one area high up in the mountains where the ground was covered in a thick bed of moss, through which animals had cut a trail so neat it looked as if it had been clipped by gardeners. Animals appeared to be plentiful, and in fact one night in this new location, a tiger came to the edge of camp.

The plan eventually called for 14 cameras, but for our first trip we decided on eight. That in itself was an ambitious undertaking as each complete set weighed around 24 kilograms; with food and other essentials we had to begin with 300 kilograms of cargo. Most of this was the responsibility of two men: Samsul and Gadi. If speed were the only consideration, it would have made sense to take eight men, but we had found that there were few people who would take on this kind of work and who could be trusted not to divulge secrets. Twice before we had lost excellent locations when porters told friends in the village about a location's rattan, fertile soil or abundant fish. So we compromised on time in the interests of security and used the two best people whom we could find.

Samsul, in his mid 30s, had been with us from the first expedition in 1983 and had been hunting with Alamshah for many years before that. His knowledge of the forest perfectly complemented Alamshah's, particularly on trees, plants and lesser animals. He was also an excellent tree climber.

Gadi was barely 20 years old and was gifted with energy, enthusiasm and courage. His strength grew throughout the project, as did the volume of his laugh—so much so that it sometimes startled us in the relative silence of the forest.

Once the four of us set out, Gadi and Samsul ferried the loads between camps as Alamshah and I prepared equipment and scouted locations. After more than a week, we reached a new area. In accordance with ancient practice Alamshah prepared for a *kenduri*, a ceremony to introduce oneself to the spirits who inhabit the jungle.

The following is an account of the *kenduri*, taken directly from my diary.

*October 22, 1987, 6.50 a.m.:* Last night, we started work on the *kenduri* preparations. Alamshah began by making a good fire and heating the freshly cleaned cooking pot. While he was waiting for the pot to reach the right temperature, he made a stiff brush from split rattan, and brushed the inside of the pot. Then taking successive handfuls of *padi pulut* (glutinous rice), he blessed them by waving them in front of his face and silently offering a prayer, and then tossed the unhusked rice into the pot. He stirred the grains for a few seconds until they started popping, replaced the lid to prevent the grains from escaping, and after a few more seconds he took off the lid and poured the jumping contents onto a dish. We now had the local equivalent of popcorn, though more delicious I might say, as I helped myself to a few stray pieces.

As Alamshah did several more batches of popped rice, we sorted through the earlier batches, removing all husks remaining on the rice—for this food was to be presented to the spirits of the location and only the best would do. If the spirits refused the offering, that could have bad repercussions.

After cooking the popped rice, Alamshah and Samsul carefully sliced some betel nut and smeared powdered lime on several sirih leaves, which are used as a wrapping for the sliced nut.

This morning Alamshah and Samsul killed the larger of the chickens. Samsul did the plucking and wasted very little in the cleaning process. Gizzard, intestines, heart and liver were all saved and will be eaten later on. A coconut has been grated and now Gadi is grinding up chili, using half a coconut shell for a mortar and a short thick stick for a pestel. Samsul is now cooking the rice.

Rather pathetically, the young cock whose friend has just met her end is making its first attempts at crowing. Perhaps it misses its companion.

*11.50 a.m.:* After the chicken was cooked, Samsul, on instructions from Alamshah, carefully wrapped up several spoonfuls of rice in large green leaves and bound the wrapping with finely split rattan.

He did the same with four bananas, a hardboiled egg and several pieces of chicken—carefully selecting a leg and claw, a piece of liver, gizzard, breast and the entire head. Then collecting all pieces together, Alamshah put them in a pandan basket and with me carrying a few smoldering coals, the two of us set off through the forest.

On the way we stopped only to scrape leeches off our legs. At last Alamshah found a dark recess of forest where he built a small altar of four upright sticks and several horizontal ones. On this simple platform, in a basket of banana leaves, he placed first the rice, then the chicken, and then the popped rice. At each of the four corners he placed the bananas cut at both ends, and the cone-shaped wrappings of betel nut. In the middle, on top, he placed the egg.

He motioned me to give him the coals, which he placed beneath the altar, then blew into flames. Then I moved away.

He squatted at the altar, and I could hear from a distance his soft chanting. As time drew on, over the peaty smell of the forest, I could detect the sweet smell of smoke from the burning of a fragrant resin. It came and went with those subtle breezes that eddy through the forest even on the calmest of days.

After half an hour or so, during which the calls of gibbon and siamangs and the falling of branches were the only sounds,

Alamshah appeared beside me. Together we returned to camp in utter silence.

Having placated the gods, we could begin the real work. The weather had been fine for a week, so I decided to capitalize on it and go as fast as possible to one of the headwaters of the Bengkung watershed. We all had loads, but Gadi's and Samsul's were particularly heavy—over 50 kilograms each. My load probably didn't exceed 25 kilograms but I was carrying the second live chicken, since Alamshah intended to perform another *kenduri* in the headwaters.

The trip turned out to be difficult and it took five days, rather than the expected two, to reach our destination. The river was constantly flooded, the weather was appalling and leeches were ravenous. I again quote from my diary.

*October 25, 1987, 11.30 a.m.:* Last night it rained steadily. We could see that the river was rising even before the rain hit us, so we moved camp in the darkness to a higher but less comfortable spot.

This morning the river was still up but clear enough for us to walk up and ford. In fact 50% of our traveling today has been in the river. For a while the weather lifted, but now it threatens to rain again and the atmosphere is dismal.

The leeches here are fierce today, especially the leaf leeches, which have an olive-green dorsal stripe and a lateral yellow line running along each side of the body. They hurt when they attach themselves, usually going for the upper leg or crotch. They are particularly difficult to remove and leave an irritable swelling.

None of us has much conversation left.

*5.45 p.m.:* This is a kingdom of damp and darkness. Already we need to light the lamp to see. The sound of rapids drowns out all noise except the high-pitched whistling of frogs and the singing of dusk cicadas nearby. Giant wild ginger plants span this torrent. Clouds merge with mist, which in turn merges with the spray of the rapids.

We are now on the upper reaches of the Bengkung, having taken the right fork shortly after lunch when torrential rain threatened to prevent us from making any progress at all. We walk in the water almost all the time now, battling against continual rapids, getting what grip we can on the slippery rocks and using our sticks at every step. Great tree trunks fallen over the river frequently bar our way. Sometimes we climb over and sometimes we crawl under, if the space between water and wood is sufficient. Vines hang from most of the trees, and orchids are prolific. Some of the leaves are huge—one like the traditional Adam and Eve fig leaf measures 60 × 45 centimeters.

We have netted another dozen fish, so that will take care of dinner tonight and perhaps breakfast tomorrow.

I'm sure that the dried fish is what gives us all the infected tongue and throat. (The ailment was probably the beginning of scurvy, which was avoided on subsequent expeditions by taking vitamin pills.)

Today the strong and normally sure-footed Gadi fell into a patch of *jelatang* (a giant stinging nettle that inflicts searing pain, which is greatly aggravated by contact with water). Although he must feel the pain dreadfully, he still uses his endless supply of energy to look for firewood, help build the *pondok*, do the cooking and help light the fire. What an asset he is!

Distant thunder continues to roll as it has done most of the afternoon. I noticed that my traveling companion, the chicken, is unusually quiet when I carry him over water. Only when we venture on to dry land does he feel at home enough to chortle.

Today Samsul fell in the river, flooding his cigarette lighter. Gadi has used up all his matches, so it is now up to the emergency supply to carry us through. We are also low on kerosene and have about six to seven full days' rations left—and we are still at least two days away from our destination.

The river is flooding as well. It suddenly rose half an hour ago and turned from its normal clarity to a dirty tea-with-a-little-milk. At the moment it's impassable.

We have made a good camp here. The fire is going well, the *tikar* are still dry (amazingly) and the fish are simmering in the *kwali*. It continues to rain but we are dry and on the whole O.K.

*October 27, 1987:* Another hard day. We have just made camp in a deep gorge filled with a real cataract. We rigged up the shelter in the last remnants of light during a torrential downpour. Everything is wet and it is taking all our combined skill to get a fire going. We use paper-thin wafers of hardwood (wet, of course) with finely chipped amber. Some kapok dipped in kerosene also helps.

We had intended to make it to the *pondok* (or the remains of what Alamshah and Gadi used on their survey trip) at the base of the location, but the weight of the packs carried by Samsul and Gadi slowed them down so much we just couldn't make it. Still, these men are expected to perform delicate balancing acts along thin branches over rapids or over maliciously slippery boulders below white water. No wonder they can go no farther.

The roar of the rapids is such that I cannot even hear the chicken's screaming (or whatever he does when terrified).

It has been white water all day except for a stretch just upstream of the waterfall above the second forks. There, a vast tree fall, extending for about half a kilometer along both sides of the gorge and choking the river with trees and debris, slowed the water down somewhat. A fierce wind must have funneled through the gorge during the last few weeks.

*Right: En route to country untouched by other humans.
Camps were simple affairs and the meager diet, where
possible, was augmented by fish. Overleaf: Moss forests in the
mountains are normally wreathed in fog.
Second spread: A flooded, impassable river.*

Short on supplies and weather-bound in the upper reaches of the river, we never did get the cameras set up on that trip. We first had to find a new route through the mountains to avoid the river. That expedition was tough, and for Christmas dinner we had to extract water from vines in order to cook rice.

When we finally reached our destination, we discovered a world quite unlike the one we had left in the lowlands. It was cold here, the trees were smaller and created the effect of a European woodland rather than a tangled jungle. On the exposed ridges, the trees were mostly twisted and draped with perpetually damp moss, but here and there small fir trees grew, appearing youthful in contrast to the bearded trees. The birds too were different from the lowland varieties, and flowers, though small, were more abundant. Mist constantly swirled around, and I must admit that this almost silent world seemed more suitable for fairies and goblins than for man.

But men had been here. After days of seeing no evidence of human beings, we found near the top of one of the highest peaks a tree blazed with some names—one read "Selah 1936." That was the most recent evidence of man we found.

I felt that animals too would not visit such a place, but I was proved wrong, for this area of high land was the center of some vast tracts of lower forest, and migrating animals frequently passed here. The place eventually became one of our most productive locations.

During the next year we made eight major expeditions into the interior. Each lasted more than three weeks and I do not remember any of them being easy. All of us suffered from sprained muscles and strained tendons, and most broke bones as well (my total was four broken ribs). Elephants sometimes destroyed our food stores, causing us periods of temporary starvation. Flooded rivers resulted in frustrating delays or forced us to search for new and frequently hazardous routes through the mountains. But despite these physical problems, our spirits remained buoyant and with each expedition I learned a little more of the forest and the lives of the creatures it harbored. This knowledge, together with what we'd gained in earlier trips over the past two years, began to reveal a series of subtle seasons that mark the passage of the forest year. The pattern may well be repeated in other areas of forest, though the timing may be different. For instance, it appears that the onset of the various fruiting seasons occurs later as the altitude increases.

Rain falls almost throughout the year in Northern Sumatra but the wettest season begins in September. Soon after these rains begin, the forest floor turns into a garden of mushrooms and other fungi—reds, yellows, black and white. The shapes vary from amorphous to dish-shaped, some like goblets and still others like hair nets. This event, which lasts only a few weeks, is an impor-

tant marker because the cats (tigers, clouded leopard and golden cat) all cover the important trails in their respective ranges more frequently. The period possibly marks an increase in their mating activity, which may peak around November, though I have recorded paired tigers as late as January. I have records of other animals, namely bear and barking deer, associating in pairs at this time also, so I wonder if the period is equivalent to springtime in the rainforest.

Coinciding with this is the beginning of the fruiting season. *Puntoh* ripen first in August, followed by several kinds of mangoes, *pangeh*, durian and *rambutan*. Several types of wild citrus fruit, including a bright-yellow lemon and a long green one, fall over a longer period from August to January. Another important crop is the wild *pateh* bean, which ripens in September.

The period from August to December is also the peak of the courting season of the argus pheasant. These birds are the size of peacocks and though lacking the latter's brilliant plumage, they do have the characteristic "eye" design on their tail feathers. When the male is ready to mate, he cleans leaves and twigs away from his traditional display ground, an area of hard, bare earth two to three meters in diameter. If his calls succeed in attracting females, he performs a "dance." If his display satisfies a discerning female, he then mates with her.

In January the noise of cicadas is so loud that one sometimes has difficulty hearing. Each evening, greenish-brown cicadas climb from the ground up the first sapling or vertical stick they can find, and later during the night they metamorphose into handsome grass-green cicadas.

It is shortly after this that the first elephants (usually small groups of cows with their young) return from distant parts of the forest to a traditional mating ground. In February they are joined by solitary bulls arriving from widely disparate areas. By May the height of the mating season is over and the bulls return "home," while the cows and their young continue on to other areas.

From June through August the weather becomes increasingly drier. Few animals, except for the occasional barking deer, are to be seen; even on major game trails, perhaps only two large animals will pass each month. For a while the forest seems asleep and then, when the rains set in, the whole cycle begins again.

It is a rare event indeed to see a Sumatran tiger in the wild and rarer still to take a satisfactory photo of one. Even the use of remote cameras does not guarantee success, for apart from potential problems with the hardware, one needs considerable knowledge to predict where the animal might be found and, equally important, in which direction it will be moving.

In view of these difficulties, even brief views of wild tigers are precious, and even more so are the photos that allow us to look at a regal animal at ease in its natural home.

All the large animals I saw or photographed in the rainforests had their special brands of beauty and their own characters. And all those sightings, either on film or in the flesh, I considered to be privileged glimpses—rare and special images that compensated for the long months of toil and enabled me to share with others something of the excitement of the forest and its denizens.

I always felt a great sense of anticipation as I drew freshly developed film from the processor. The film rolls already had a history. They had been carried to distant locations and had been left in a camera for weeks on end. This was followed by a two-week trek out of the mountains and back to civilization, and then finally back to Medan and the studio. I never knew exactly what to expect because many animals would pass by a location without leaving any detectable sign. But if everything had worked as planned, when I held the film up to the light, it would reveal moments in the lives of real animals.

Many of these animals are rare now, but they were not always so. Up until 1984, tigers were still common in southern Aceh, particularly near the town of Ladang Rimba where I stayed for a while as a guest of the local *Koramil*, Pak Ali. Tigers would sometimes pass by Ali's home. In fact, one did so while I was there. Ali had many tiger stories and one stimulated my interest. It was of a woman in a village near the town of Labuan Haji who could call tigers from the hills.

Being somewhat of a cynic, I decided to investigate at first hand, so shortly thereafter the two of us went to the lady's village—a neat collection of houses situated at the base of forested hills that descend to the west Aceh coastal plain. The woman consented to call a tiger but suggested we come back two nights later in order to give the tiger time to respond. We did so and learned to our chagrin that a tiger had come on cue the previous night. Several villagers had seen it and excitedly told me their own versions.

I cursed my luck but the lady assured me that the tiger would still be around, so we waited for nightfall. I quickly learned that although I might be interested in seeing tigers, the villagers were more interested in me. As I drank coffee and fielded questions from the elders of the village, the children crammed around the windows to look inside. The curiosity continued well into the night. Short of insulting the hospitality of these kind people, there was no way I could leave to wait for a wary tiger.

As the night wore on, the numbers of people thinned out. I was hoping to join the lady when a great commotion erupted from a house only 50 meters away. Ali and I raced across to discover that a tiger had walked into the kitchen of the house and begun scratching on the door of the sleeping quarters. When one of the men opened the door, he was so shocked that he screamed and frightened the tiger away.

Hoping for a photograph, I persuaded the lady to call one more time, so together with Ali the three of us made our way to a stream at the end of the village. There, some time after midnight, the lady unwrapped a cake of rice and food, laid it on a grass mat and began incanting in a high voice, concluding with some loud whistling. The tiger, no doubt still frightened, did not come again, so after a couple of hours we retired to bed.

Although the local people consider such acts to be the work of magic, there may be a more prosaic explanation.

Years ago, the lady had a dream in which two orphaned kittens approached her and begged for food. She consented and the kittens expressed their gratitude. The next day while working in her *ladang* (a garden in a forest clearing), she saw two tigers at the forest's edge. Recognizing the significance of her dream, she prepared food and left it at the place where she saw the tigers, whistling as she left. After that she continued to leave food out, and periodically the tigers came to eat—perhaps learning to associate her call and whistle with the opportunity for easy food.

The people of southern Aceh seemed to accept that the tigers helped to keep down the depradations of pigs that would normally eat their crops. A relatively high number of tigers existed there until outsiders began to poison them in 1984. Few tigers ate people and those that did were normally trapped and killed. I met one man who had been attacked by a tiger and escaped. The man was fishing in a slow-moving river that runs to the town of Truman. Standing waist deep in the water, with just his head visible from the bank, he must have seemed like easy prey to the tiger that happened to be nearby. The tiger had crept up behind the fisherman before the man sensed that something was wrong. On turning around he saw the tiger as it attacked like a cat pouncing on a mouse. The two fell into the water, and after almost tearing the man's scalp off, the tiger released his grip and swam away. Two friends who were nearby helped the man back to his village, then washed and bandaged his head. Three weeks later he was fully recovered except for the deep scars he still bears.

Curiously enough, the man has no hatred of tigers and even claims to have a certain affinity with them.

During our expeditions, tigers would sometimes approach our camp, but after a cursory inspection they would make a detour and carry on with their business.

One night though, around 3 a.m., during a period of light rain, a tiger approached within 12 meters of camp and spent a long time observing us. We shouted at it a few times and it retreated a few paces only to settle down again. It would have been interesting to observe him for a while but our flashlight batteries were low and we were exhausted from several days of very tiring work, so we soon went back to sleep. Before dawn, he was gone.

The most curious episode, however, occurred shortly after Samsul and Sukiman had had their close encounter with a tiger while collecting durians. On this occasion, they and another assistant, Amat, were traveling to the Air Putih river to collect some equipment, when they discovered that a tiger was following them down the trail. Being weighed down with heavy loads and fully aware they could never outrun the tiger, they just kept walking. Sometimes the tiger would vanish and then reappear, walking parallel to the men some distance off through the trees, or sometimes walking along the trail up ahead. In all, these appearances lasted for more than an hour.

For some reason, Samsul and Amat decided that Sukiman was in league with the tiger and therefore highly dangerous. So that night they secretly arranged that he should sleep between them in order to prevent him from getting up to mischief with his striped friend.

Samsul and Amat were so concerned about the incident that they threatened to quit unless Sukiman was fired. Since they were both excellent workers, I subsequently had Sukiman replaced with another man.

These incidents convinced me that tigers are not the ruthless man-eaters they are sometimes depicted to be. Indeed, man is not the normal prey of the tiger. Near the forest's edge pigs constitute the main part of the tiger's diet and in the forest, where pigs tend to be fewer, the tiger favors rusa deer and kijang.

During our travels in the forest we saw kijang on several occasions. When alarmed, they would repeatedly jump up with tails erect and land on the ground with a ponking sound. As they ran off, they would give a few sharp barks, followed by a long roar that was repeated many times until the deer considered itself out of harm's way.

Rusa are much more wary, especially by day, and much less common than the kijang. When we disturbed one near a thicket of bamboo, the animal took off at a frantic speed, its head and neck outstretched to facilitate its rapid passage through the undergrowth. In photographs I took, I noticed that sometimes the animal had a sore on its throat, which may have been caused by hitting vines in the understory.

Rusa are delicious to eat and much sought after. Tigers presumably agree, for we frequently found rusa remains in their scats. Despite this, tigers don't always succeed and the two times I recorded tigers chasing rusa through the forest, the rusa were able to get away.

The tiger also preys on the serow—an unusual animal that looks somewhat like a large goat and is covered in glossy black hair. Serow live in the most rugged country and have a special liking for limestone areas, which provide dry shelter and some protection against predators. At least near their homes, serow follow regular paths, and I have seen rocks on which there is a smooth strip polished by the passage of many serow hooves. They are also quite willing to enter small caves and narrow crevices—such as one place that was difficult for us to squeeze into, but which contained a deliquescent crystalline vein that the animals liked to lick. Serow also insist on clean places to rest and sleep—often choosing flat stones in inaccessible places. Before settling down, they will blow any dust and dirt away, much as domestic goats will, and in places that are regularly used, this wall of dust surrounding the clean resting area may be two centimeters high. In fact, the sleeping places are polished smooth with long use and all that one can find are a few of the animals' black hairs.

At such resting places I have found fresh tiger tracks. The places are so inaccessible that we had to approach one by climbing vines and aerial roots, and I can only assume the tiger visited the place, expecting to find serow.

Above all, tigers are opportunists and I have found in their scats the remains of porcupine, orang-utan and even a rat.

Besides tigers, we saw some of the other carnivores in the course of our expeditions—otter, bears and wild dogs. Wild dogs are rare in Sumatra and we saw them only once. On that occasion we were making good progress along a well-used but leech-infested elephant trail when an explosion of high-pitched barks broke out just ahead of us. Whatever made the noise ran off, but less than a minute later the squealing and barking passed us again and moved around us. It sounded like three animals, one of which gave a high-pitched whine or whistle. Eventually, one of the animals showed itself—a reddish-brown dog with a fox-like tail. In a second it was gone, leaving just the memory of a frustratingly fleeting glimpse of a rare forest animal.

Bears, on the other hand, are not as excitable as dogs and are more easily seen. Once when traveling with only Gadi as a companion deep in the mountains, I came across a large bear. He had already sensed my approach but would not be hurried and slowly ambled ahead for several hundred yards, casually looking back to check on me. I remember the way his fur rippled as he walked off, as if he were wearing a heavy coat over a layer of jelly.

The Malay sun bear, which is found throughout South East Asia, eats a wide variety of foods from bees' nests to beetles and berries, but in the mountains I found that about 60% of their scats had resin and amber remains in them. Since the bear does not eat this by accident, I can only assume he derives some nutritional value from it.

Many animals that we never saw showed up on film—among them, civets, pangolin, martens, the rare golden cat and the clouded leopard. The cats are special because they represent a beauty rarely seen. Of the men, only Samsul had seen a clouded leopard. On that occasion it was lying on a branch high up on a fig tree, and its camouflage matched the background so well that when Samsul moved his eyes he had difficulty finding it again. None of us ever saw a golden cat and little seems to be known about them. In fact, few local people even know of its existence.

The golden cat with its relatively long legs and short tail is probably a predominantly terrestrial animal, and is capable of covering large areas. The one shown in this book covered an area at least five kilometers long and two kilometers wide. In my experience, their altitudinal range reaches from upper lowland forest to at least 1,700 meters and in this range its prey includes large ground birds such as the argus pheasant and wood partridge.

The clouded leopard is a creature ideally suited to the trees. Low-slung, with large feet and a tail almost a meter long, it is well adapted to an arboreal existence. Its coat is the last word in camouflage and for this reason it may be successful in hunting primates. According to researchers at Ketambe, the macaques there were more alarmed by a clouded leopard than by any other creature. Yet for all its skill in the trees, it covers great distances on the ground, and I found the same leopard in locations 10 kilometers apart.

Eventually there was one animal whose sign we frequently saw but which we never photographed. That was the Sumatra rhino. In our last 10 expeditions we saw fresh tracks on all but two. Yet the animal, like a phantom, eluded our best efforts. It is already rare and as development goes ahead, its home shrinks. For us it remains a symbol of the forests and a reminder that, though we partially lifted the veil, some animals still guard their privacy and some secrets still remain.

*Right:* The wild boar is less common in primary forest than near settlements, and freed from the constraints imposed by human activity is frequently active by day.
*Below:* The rainforests of South East Asia are rich in civet cats such as this masked palm civet.

*The wary and elusive crested wood partridge*

*Left: The serow is rarely seen because it prefers rugged, inaccessible country. Below: The binturong, the largest of Sumatra's civets, is primarily arboreal, but occasionally forages on the ground.*

*Wallowing is a popular activity of both the rusa deer and pig.*

*Right: The golden cat is one of the most secretive of animals, almost always nocturnal and probably terrestrial—to judge by its long legs and short tail. Below: The furtive kijang is constantly alert to predators such as the tiger.*

*The clouded leopard, a master of camouflage, is rarely seen by man.*

*The tiger, the greatest predator in the Sumatran forest, is becoming increasingly rare.*